WAKE UP

WAKE UP

Chemical Dependency Family Interventions

Eileen Wolfe

To order additional copies of this book, contact:
Xlibris Corporation
1-888-795-4274
www.Xlibris.com
Orders@Xlibris.com

40111

Contents

Dedication

I dedicate this book to my deceased father, Edward Martin Davis. He was an alcoholic since I was born and only in his hospital bed before he died did he listen to AA members who came to visit him.

He died at 62 years of age just before his retirement. I hope this book can offer recovery to family members, friends, and alcoholics/addicts.

I want to thank by beloved husband, Edward Wolfe for his encouragement. To my son George Nomikos for bringing laughter when I wanted to give up and for my daughters, Margarita Nomikos and Christine Wolfe for asking are you done yet?

Well I have completed this book and I hope more will follow.

The final thank you is the most important and this is to my higher power, which I call God. Hopefully together we can gain recovery for this disease called chemical dependency earlier.

Biography

Eileen Mary Davis was born in Brooklyn and was raised as an only child in Richmond Hill Queens to an alcoholic father and a raging mother. Eileen enjoyed times when her father brought her to his large family gatherings as well as the closeness to her Aunt Margaret Davis. Eileen attended Catholic grammar school/high school as well as receiving a full scholarship for nursing school at Queens General School of Nursing. She worked as a nurse for four years including becoming the assistant head nurse of the OB/GYN clinic at Queens General Hospital. She went to work during the daytime and attended classes at NYIT for community mental health at night. Later she completed her master's degree in Social Work at Adelphi University School of Social Work in 1982. She married in the interim and adopted two beautiful children and after 19 years of marriage she asked her husband for a divorce. She remarried 6 years later and she is happily married and living in Albertson Long Island New York with her husband while her son is away at college but calls her home "base". Her daughter and stepdaughter live independently and are also attending school.

Eileen is a member of the Association for Intervention Specialists AIS. She is currently an interventionist, motivational speaker, and educator, writer and in private practice on Long Island New York.

Everyday she is learning different ways to intervene on the family dynamics of Chemical Dependency. She is versed in the Johnson, and Systemic models of intervention and now opening her mind to others such as the Storki and Arise models of intervention.

It is important for the general public to learn that there is a new certification for interventionist called AISBB. I believe that those people who qualify for this certification will be top of the line interventionists which should be chosen in order to gain qualified providers to perform interventions.

Introduction

This book is for anyone who know or whose family member has a problem with alcohol and other drugs. It is sad to receive a call from an 83 year old mom in recovery in Alcoholics Anonymous with one son just getting out of detox and another son in denial of his drug problem who was just fired from his employment.

It is frustrating to hear treatment professionals lacking knowledge about chemical dependency interventions and unknowingly blocking family members from moving ahead to break the denial of the addicted family member or friend.

My desire is to educate one person at a time in order to intervene earlier on the drinking alcoholic and drugging addict as well as the family members and friends.

You see perhaps, in the future I could imagine that the next 83 year old mom in recovery in AA for thirty years would be able to offer interventions to her children much earlier, so that her adult children would be on a path of recovery from the family disease and when or if they become alcoholics/addicts themselves it would be addressed much sooner.

Yes, professional interventions have been done for years. Many have been successful in getting the active alcoholic/addict to start abstaining one day at a time; some have not. What is the missing link? There is no education for the entire family/friends to increase a higher level of recovery for the active alcoholic/addict and to start the process of intergenerational family recovery of the family disease of chemical dependency. Also, to identify other family members who are active in all kinds of other addictions such as gambling, eating disorders etc and help them gain recovery.

Some of you may be confused about the family disease of chemical dependency. To clarify, the alcoholic/addict is addicted to their chemical and the family members/friends are addicted to the alcoholic/addict. Even to the point they talk incessantly about them as if they were living in their alcoholic/addict's body. Eventually they don't exist individually and live only to try and stop the alcoholic/addict from taking their drug of choice. This family disease of co-dependency can make them physically, emotionally, psychologically and spiritually ill by increasing the levels of stress the family members/friends place on themselves. This is in addition to the stress placed on them they think by the behavior of their alcoholic/addict loved ones.

Typical Calls

1. A sister is drinking and drugging round the clock and she has three children under the age of 5. Her husband is at his wits end. How can you help me asks the husband?
2. A call from a daughter living in California about her elderly mom living with her drug abusing adult son in New York. Please help.
3. My elderly father who has landed again in the intensive care unit due to yet another fall in which he was intoxicated. Please help.
4. A call from an elderly couple, afraid for their lives, trapped and abused by their adult addict son living with them. Softly but desperately they say please help.
5. A call from the mother of a teenage daughter who has been suspended from school and refuses to do anything to address her daughter's chemical dependency. Please help.
6. A call from a wife whose husband has promised to quit drinking many times and had a really bad night. He wrecked the house and now is in jail since the police were called. Please help.
7. A call from a father about his college son in his senior year at an Ivy League college and has been expelled due to his drug dealing. Please help.
8. My wife relapsed after ten years of sobriety after our son was just killed. Please help.
9. A call from a friend whose other friend's child confided in her about the little girl's parents'daily drinking and drugging. The little girl is 6 years old. Please help.
10. A call from a college roommate who three weeks ago experienced the death of a freshman from an alcohol overdose and now is afraid for another college freshman. Please help.

11. A call from a woman who has again been physically and verbally abused by her lover. Please help.

The calls above are a few possible account from people like you who are stressed about the alcoholic/addict's behavior in your life. It can get better. You must become open-minded and courageous to consider a chemical dependency intervention. If I accomplish this in my book I have succeeded. As they say in Alcoholics Anonymous(for the alcoholics and Al-anon(for the family members/friends of the alcoholic) "You are responsible for the effort, but not the outcome."

Chemical Dependency is a primary, chronic, progressive but most importantly treatable disease. As the disease progresses in the alcoholic/addict it follows suit in the family members/friends who are not addicted to any chemicals.

So make an effort to read this book and take action to call an interventionist so you can start your family recovery. Please note certified interventionists who belong to AIS and are certified by AISCB are reviewed for the highest regards in terms of ethics and experience and training. Please start with selecting an interventionist from that provider list.

The Family Disease of Chemical Dependency

Family members and friends are preoccupied with their alcoholic/addict and appear to be living and breathing within them. When a family member enters my office and constantly talks about their alcoholic/addict instead of listening to my questions and doesn't answer the questions at all I know I have a severe case of co-dependency in front of me. That person or persons are my first clients, not the alcoholic/addict they have come to talk about. These clients often accept unacceptable behavior that others would run from because they have developed increased tolerance of unacceptable behavior. Recently, a father arrived in my office and described how his son 42 years old got into treatment even though he was in my office for his 34 year old heroin addicted daughter. He described how his son burned his house down last year and nearly killed the whole family. Finally, his son went for help. He had given his daughter $28,000.00 last year and could no longer afford to take care of her. He wanted to know what could be done for her. For finishers he described that is wife at 79 years old just stopped drinking cold turkey. This elderly man who was my first client had developed an increased tolerance for the unacceptable behavior from his wife, son and daughter. Physically he was hunched over and worn emotionally. His eyes appeared sunken and his enthusiasm for life was long gone many years ago. He lost his control by probably attempting to control the uncontrollable. Many times family members describe their bizarre behavior to stop the alcoholic/addict from getting or doing their drug of choice. We know the usual like throwing the liquor down the sink or putting water in the vodka bottle or marking how much is left in the bottle. What about driving around the neighborhood with the kids in the back seat looking for the alcoholic for hours totally forgetting the children are even in the car. We all know about what I call drug heaven, when enablers feed clothe, shelter their alcoholic/addict every day as well as supplying them money for their drugs. What about taking away the alcoholic/addict's car because their loved one was drinking/drugging and driving, but allowing their alcoholic/addict to drive a motorcycle drunk. To top it off the enablers even paid for the gas and insurance on that motorcycle.

The reason for this bizarre behavior of the enablers is that their denial is extremely strong and impermeable. Also, they the family members/friends are not frozen in suspension by a chemical so the raw emotion is exhibited and often other family members look upon those who are not addicted as sometimes crazier than the alcoholic/addict themselves. The family disease of chemical dependency has a foundation of unacceptable behavior as well. Therefore, each one of us involved in the drama of chemical dependency must be willing to look clearly at ourselves and make the necessary changes to acceptable behavior before pointing fingers at the alcoholics/addicts. An example of denial that is life threatening is an adult son allowed his active alcoholic mom to drive his kids to school every day for four years and now is worried because one of his neighbors complained and told him they would call the authorities if it continued even one more day. Why did an educated loving father/son do such a thing? Denial that it wasn't that bad and the rationalization that he didn't have anyone else since his wife left with another man four years ago kept him stuck.

Medical problems in family members are numerous and many times extreme. Constant stress place on themselves and the stress with the interaction of their alcoholic/addict places havoc on all the organs of their body. Hopefully they will learn to stop the stress they placed on themselves and learn to deal with the interaction between them and their alcoholic/addict.

Financially families are drained in the family disease. Case in point is a wealthy elderly couple in an affluent area on Long Island in which they lost their mom and pop deli and then their home due to all the money they gave or allowed their alcoholic/addict to steal with no consequences. They left with their alcoholic/addict roaming the streets and they not having enough money for their daily necessities.

What about all the events we hear in the media when the addict abuses or kills their children? Sometimes the family members/friends themselves accept unacceptable behavior for years. Other times those supposedly sane people attack their alcoholics/addicts and kill them. Both sides are wrong. We must stop this senseless acts of violence whether planned or happening in a rage from the alcoholic/addict or family/friends.

The shame associated with what is occurring behind closed doors is immense. Of course, I am speaking of all kinds of abuse, but the tolerance for it gets progressively worse just like the alcoholic/addict's tolerance for their drug of choice increases and is more frequent. Family members and friends enter psychiatric facilities just like their addict because their psyche is just as fragile. Spiritually there is either an emptiness that is eerie or a false fantasy that everything is all right. A higher power is either nonexistent or acting as a superman without any common sense action on their part to help their higher power along. I could write forever on this topic, but I need to address the reason why I assess the clients that are first presented in my office. I must ascertain if I have a healthy enough family to begin the intervention process. If not I stop the intervention despite the frantic call from the family. I request the family and friends to immediately attend the appropriate 12 step program and to start or continue with therapists specializing in chemical dependency. Sometimes the family is too raw and bleeding emotionally themselves.

So in that case I ask two family/friends that have arrived at the intervention assessment to go for therapy for co-dependency and attend on a regular basis the correct 12 step program. I usually schedule another session in the near future to see if they have followed my suggestion and then look to see if they are starting to heal from the family disease of chemical dependency. Then and only then do I proceed. It is imperative that the family recognize their part in the disease an be willing to change in order to increase the chances for their alcoholic/addict to start and continue their own recovery. You see the ideal scenario is that all members of the family are actively involved in their own 12 step program. Everyone in the family speaks the same language and supports recovery not the disease.

When I hear and see a family my heart cries out for them and sometimes I cry after they leave and pray for them. I feel that my job brings me to the war zone of the disease of chemical dependency. On the other hand, at times I have met very healthy families and felt joyous to catalyze the healing of their addicted family member. This type of situation is easy for me the social worker and easier for the alcoholic/addict. Still the alcoholic/addict can not neglect their own recovery work even though their family is so healthy.

You see some families have a strong foundation with which to build on in recovery and others have no or little foundation due to the generational addiction issues. Both families can be helped. It just takes one a little longer to ground the recovery. Also, the strong healthy family can crumble after a couple of generations of addictions in the future. So healthy families can't say to themselves, "I don't need that psychobabble because the disease of chemical dependency can disseminate a family." Believe me I have seen the destruction.

Destruction includes physical, and verbal abuse by one or all parties, physical squalor, unspeakable sexual abuse etc. The reason why I say etc is that I don't intend to discuss those issues in detail. This is not a tabloid. The disease of chemical dependency is a war zone that can be restored to health one person at a time one day at a time. What does it take? First, it takes ownership that there is an alcoholic/addict in your home and then start your own recovery and ask your alcoholic/addict to join you in your recovery during perhaps a professionally planned intervention.

Money, where does it come from? Before families come to an interventionist they have been enabling their alcoholics/addicts for years. The lack of money comes about due to the family disease of chemical dependency when they will do absolutely anything even go broke to save their alcoholic/addict. They think if I can take care of his/her debt they the addict will have less stress, therefore, they won't drink or drug. You see and alcoholic/addict uses if the day is sunny or if it is rainy. If they want to use their drug of choice they will no matter what. Stop the money flow. Stop preventing the natural consequences of your alcoholic/addict's behavior from affecting them. Stop taking the hit yourselves every time.

Those of you who are reading this book and wondering, "Can I afford an intervention or can I afford to support my alcoholic/addict emotionally in recovery?" I can repeat what is stated in the 12 step rooms, "You can do it one day at a time." Things can be figured out and talked about within the family.

In recovery I have heard alcoholics/addicts repay their families for the intervention performed on them. I have witnessed families pooling their resources and having an intervention in place of paying for a future wedding gift or college education. A more important possible gift of sobriety can be offered. I also have seen the offering of interventions pro bono once in a while for those in need and also wealthy philanthropists donate their money for families in need of interventions.

What Does Alcoholism Look Like?

Well, we know a major symptom is loss of control ie "I make a promise to myself to have 2 beers at the bar and that is all I have. The next time I go out I make the same promise and I get drunk. The third time I go out I state again to myself I am only going to have 2 beers and I have 2 beers. The fourth consecutive time I go out and make the same promise and get drunk. Then I stop drinking for a while and then go back to the drinking as usual more regularly even though I have made a promise to myself I would only have 2 beers. "I really don't' want to do it just happens." This is called progressive loss of control. Eventually as the disease progresses there is never a time for just a few beers.

What I think is that a young child starts drinking at age 12 and by 16 sometimes are really addicted not just abusing alcohol and other drugs. Parents sometimes ignore their child's behavior until the consequences of their teenager is affecting that child and other children as well as the rest of the family. It is hard to imagine the diagnosis of chemical dependency in their teenager. Sometimes teenagers are abusing and not addicted, but will get what they paid for—chemical dependency. Note interventions should should be done for chemical dependency not use, misuse or abuse. Many people might say, "Well my son is just experimenting like his friends. "90% of the time when I speak to adolescents they tell the truth about the amount and kind of alcohol/drugs they are using if they are interested in getting help. Usually it is 80% more than what the parents suspect. It is hard also for parents to accept that "Little Johnny" is really doing those things we hear on the news.

Other times parents are knowledgeable and do the alcohol/drugs with their children. A case in point was when a mother approached me about her cocaine addicted son who did lines of cocaine with his father who was a practicing medical doctor. We first had to do an intervention on her husband before we could attempt an intervention on her son.

A third scenario is that knowledgeable parents offer their children the help they need, but the child makes an attempt at recovery just to placate his/her parents. Meanwhile, downward progression of the disease continues and it is very sad especially when parents are faced with the death of their child. Jail time, many inpatient psychiatric hospital admissions and still sometimes their child does not gain the courage to change.

Many people hear of all the celebrity children or the celebrities are not in solid recovery despite all the treatment they receive. Unfortunately, people don't hear about the great recovery of children and adults. There is a young people's AA meeting on Long Island, New York that is active. There are many treatment facilities that have strong alumni associations that remain clean and sober. There are many mature adults who received the gift of sobriety when they were young adults and are still in strong recovery today.

What Does Alcoholism Look Like in Adulthood?

Many times family members/friends arrive for an intervention assessment because of a particular situation that was intolerable to them. That was their defining factor that they desire an intervention to be completed.

1. A call from a parent about a son who doesn't work, sleeps all day and drinks every night. Ever since 9-11 he has lost his job and got depressed. Then drank heavier and heavier until he wasn't able to pay his bills. He is living with my wife and myself and we are afraid. Please help.

2. A young adult who gets in trouble smoking marijuana at school While going through the process of suspension she experiences a drug overdose and is rushed to the hospital. Her parents never notified the school about the situation. The parents and the young adult even pretend to the counselor that the marijuana incident was her first and last time she will be involved with drugs. The family experiences the pain of the progression of the disease of chemical dependency only after she is admitted back to school, getting a 3.0 GPA, involved in activities and then it hits them all. Another consequence, this time a DWI and she is arrested. They call for help.

3. A mother calls stating her son has had four car accidents under the influence of alcohol. She claims she got him off all four times. He is now verbally abusing her and now she thinks he may have a problem. Please help.

4. A call from a wife stating her husband has lost many jobs and she works two jobs to pay their bills. Last week he physically assaulted the mailman and may have to go to jail. She states, "I think I may need an intervention done."

Usually people wait an average 20 years watching defined addicted behavior in their loved one. They usually know after the first 5 years that chemical dependency is present, but try all the family disease techniques for the next 15 years before many of them finally surrender.

You see the problem is that many times the alcoholic/addict secretly know they are an alcoholic/addict, but they don't want to give up their drug of choice. The family members usually don't speak directly to the alcoholic/addict for those first five years. Therefore, nothing is done by anyone for five years at least and then the next 15 years the family and friends try to control the alcoholic/addict as much as the alcoholic/addict tries to control his family by manipulating them to believing it is not that bad.

Progression and what is the last straw for each family is different. Some people will tolerate all types of unacceptable behavior from family members and other families will tolerate only a little. Some families don't even realize the behavior is unacceptable because in their childhood unacceptable behavior was the norm. They can't distinguish what behavior is in normal ranges. That is why Alcoholism and Drug Dependence and what it looks like varies to a person's level of tolerance for unacceptable behavior.

Well each one of you has to determine your level yourself. Many people define the physical abuse of children as a defining point, and others define the burning down of the whole house as the defining factor. At the other end of the spectrum a husband will state his wife's drinking has escalated in the loneliness he feels not having a companion is the deciding factor while another is the wife's getting evidence that her husband is having an affair with a woman while he is out drunk.

The important concept is that when you define the moment, take action by seriously thinking about your options. An action could be to calmly speak to the person the next day, not when they are drunk or high. Get information about help beforehand so in case they ask for help you will know where to take them. If they refuse don't argue with them. Solicit other family members to talk to the person individually and if the person still refuses help please consider an intervention.

What Does Intergenerational Recovery Look Like?

Recovery of one generation or more of alcoholics/addicts starts spreading backwards to the parents, grandparents, and great grandparents who also look at themselves etc. Then we look forward to the present children, aunts, uncles, cousins etc. When I first do a genogram with the family and see all the intergenerational dysfunction it is very sad. I have not ever done it, but it would be nice to see the intergenerational recovery in a family. If there are those of you with that story perhaps I could write about your family to help others understand recovery intergenerationally.

In my travels I have witnessed a son in recovery and the father went into recovery with the son's help. The father was a biker who partied hardy, but when his son started following in his father's footsteps his son was confronted by the family and he went into recovery. His father watched his son's recovery from a distance and decided to start recovery himself. The father has started a sober biker club. He has AA slogans all over his leather vest. Amazing stories.

We can have many more amazing stories if people request information and follow through on more interventions. It would be nice to have the norm healthy behavior in all ages of our society. It starts one person at a time, one day at a time.

Adult Children and Children
Before An Intervention

When an adult child of an alcoholic begins to ask family members to attend an education session in the hopes of completing an intervention, sometimes family members complain that the adult child asking the family for their time maybe unmercilessly critized. Let me give examples. Mary called after taking one year to gain the courage to start an intervention and her family remarks, "You should have done this years ago. Isn't there a way you can lock him up against his will, you were not tough enough with him, we are disgusted with him, We don't want to waste our time with him, we don't think it will work now, we don't want to be involved. etc" Other times families are eager to start and finally some families state, "They don't see him/her having a problem with alcohol/drugs."

Adult children of alcoholics or people raised by adult children of alcoholics without treatment can pass down the same attitudes and thinking processes as the active alcoholic/addict without the actual ingestion of the alcohol/drug. So when the one family member makes a sincere attempt to bring the family together for an intervention—that is a miracle if they actually follow through. Sometimes, as I mentioned before, I see a healthy family foundation, sometimes a mediocre or a severely dysfunctional family. The continued miracle is that I believe, through God's intervention, even the most dysfunctional families complete interventions and go into solid recovery. It is true I often have heard the "mayor" or the good looking person at the rehabilitation center leave and pick up their drug of choice quickly. Sometimes the slow paced recovering individual with backward slides in treatment at the rehabilitation center leave and continue with long term sobriety and abstinence. It is not what you have inherited, but what you do with what you have as the saying goes. Therefore, any family or individual can go into strong recovery.

So no matter how difficult it may seem to get your family/friends together, if they are committed, healing is possible for everyone attending.

Some families make a commitment ASAP and do the intervention well. Others have numerous intervention assessments and never complete an intervention. Finally other families plan interventions way in advance and keep canceling. I believe if the two people that came to me or spoke over the phone are not ready, I send them for assistance. Otherwise we start the process. If the family is resisting it may be a good idea to ask them to be more open-minded.

The process of an intervention may start with someone saying, "There has to be something better than this." It is that moment that change is possible.

What Happens When Your Loved One Enters Treatment?

First the family and friends must concentrate on their own recovery by attending Al-anon/Nar-anon or Families Anonymous meetings. Talking to their temporary sponsor in those 12 step programs, reading 12 step literature, selecting a homegroup in those 12 step meetings and seeking counseling, if needed. Sometimes another alcoholic/addict surfaces and the family at the second follow up session after the intervention session does a mini intervention in order to get another alcoholic/addict into treatment.

Meanwhile your first loved one may try to escape the situation to start the family disease again. Other times a person leaves early and relapses or the person stays to complete the program and relapses. Anytime the person relapses during or after treatment the family can state, "We support your recovery not your addiction." Ask the person if they want help again. If your loved one refuses lovingly say, "If you want help call otherwise you will follow through with the previous prepared consequences.

What Does Treatment
Look Like?

Interventionist associated with the Association of Intervention Specialists (AIS) and have the certification of BRI,BRII along with the AIS are the highest level of interventionist. Those professionals should be the first you consider to do your family intervention.

There are many and varied detoxification programs, including medical, nonmedical, and outpatient forms.

Rehabilitation Centers are not for profit, 12 step, therapeutic community, combination of 12 step and therapeutic community, state of the art, bare basics, dual diagnosis, multiple chemical dependency treatment, gender specific track, age specific track, professional track, adolescent track, young adult track, musicians track etc.

Halfway houses can be from 2 weeks to months, unstructured, structured, dual diagnosis etc.

Private therapy specializing in Chemical Dependency with licensed certified social workers, psychologists, alcoholism counselors, supervised by social workers or psychologists and psychiatrists specializing in Chemical Dependency.

Outpatient counseling in agencies specializing in Chemical Dependency as an intensive outpatient agency, regular outpatient agency, dual diagnosis agency, for profit and not for profit agencies.

Councils specializing in Chemical Dependency information, assessment, referral, prevention through education, coalition building, low cost interventions and some counseling is available.

Payment sometimes is through private insurance, Medicaid, Medicare, sliding scale, private pay or donations.

What Happens When Your Loved One Comes Out Of Rehabilitation?

Sometimes your loved one may enter a halfway house for a transition before returning to the world at large. Whether your loved one enters a halfway house or some other living arrangement, they are recommended to attend 90 AA/NA meetings in 90 days, get a temporary sponsor, read conferenced approved literature daily, volunteer in the 12 step program, participate in 12 step social activities after making friends in the 12 step program.

The Intervention Process

In my opinion you begin with an intervention assessment with two family members. They will be given information about different kinds of interventions. Not just the Johnson Model that is discussed in this book. You will be given different treatment facilities suitable for your loved one so you can investigate. I try to make the correct fit of your loved one to a particular few facilities depending on a number of variables. Of course, it is always has the component of a 12 step model. It is also extremely important to make sure your loved one is actually chemically dependent before we proceed. I have had occasions of a divorce proceeding in which one party waited to pin the diagnosis on the other spouse for custody issues. I spotted it and refused to do the intervention on that person.

A very important point is that my first clients are the two people I talk to on the phone, speak to through email or see in person. If those two clients are ready we start building the team for the intervention. If they are not ready I start their healing in order to strengthen them for the intervention in the future.

During the intervention assessment I decide which type of intervention model or which combination of intervention to use for each particular family. For the purpose of this book I will just talk about the Johnson Model. I ask the first two clients to begin to attend Al-anon/Nar-anon or Family Anonymous as well as counseling that specializes in Chemical Dependency. Therefore, I begin the process of acceptance on their part of having the family disease of Chemical Dependency and then I also talk about inviting their loved one into their recovering family. Their loved one is not a bad person; they are in need of recovery. If they are willing to start the intervention process and I feel I can do that particular intervention we plan a date for the education, pre-rehearsal, rehearsal, and intervention. Before the scheduled educational session the family has chosen the treatment facility for their loved one. On the day of the education session family members/friends, neighbors, clergy, and possible work personnel are invited to attend. The criteria includes people who love, like or care for the loved one you are intervening on. Remember many times your loved one's behavior pushed people away and they are angry and hurt, but they may still love him/her. Each intervention team member is expected to attend all the educational sessions including the education, pre-rehearsal, rehearsal, and the intervention. Closure and follow up sessions are encouraged.

At the time of the education each family is different. Some are willing to move forward and accept healing while others are in denial of their loved one's chemical dependency or like the status quo. Meaning they resist change within the family. Others are so weak from enabling that their own emotional energy is depleted. In that morning session of the educational day I will witness what foundation is present for continuing an intervention. Sometimes it appears nearly impossible to get it off the ground and by the afternoon of that same day the family/friends move readily along to my amazement. On a few occasions I had to stop the intervention because of the family/friends level of readiness.

During the afternoon the family/friends begin to understand their part in the continuation of the chemical dependency in their loved one. Then we start their love letter which is the core of the Johnson Model type of intervention. I usually ask them to start with, "How much they love or like their alcoholic/addict in detail?—a flashback from the past." I usually ask the parents to talk about when their loved one was born or when they were young. To imagine it, visualize it. Write it down and savor that time. The second part of the love letter is when they felt proud of their loved one. Again in detail, imagine it, visualize it and write it down so they can savor the moment themselves. I HELP FAMLY AND FRIENDS GET STARTED OR HELP THEM FINISH. Many times everyone is so enmeshed with the disasters of the present that it is very hard to realize the way the person was. I am always so happy to hear how loving, caring and giving their alcoholic/addict used to be to everyone. Therefore, so many people take time out of their ;lives to do this intervention for their loved one who is sick now.

The third part of the love letter includes one detailed situation in which their loved one's drinking/drugging affected them. Sometimes family/friends are overwhelmed and can't choose one situation. Other times they try to escape by generally speaking instead of going into detail about the situation. The fourth part of the letter is the same for all. "Please join us in recovery."

Eventually the letters are written, felt and critiqued. It is important to be concise in detail and as brief as you can be.

During the day of education I choose who will be the chairperson. He/She will start talking first by reading their love letter after everyone is seated. The interventionist first introduces themselves and explains that they have been working with the family who will speak to them now. Of course this is done after the loved one has been seated by the family. The interventionist explains further that after everyone is finished the alcoholic/addict will have a chance to speak. During the education day people on the intervention team will volunteer to pack the bag for the loved one, two others will volunteer to drive their loved one to treatment the family has chosen ahead of time.

Another volunteer will pack lunch for three people in the car as well as having a readable direction with the name, address and telephone number of the treatment facility. Those people who could not attend the day of education and would like to write a letter are asked to call the interventionist for assistance. The intervention team brainstorms during lunch during the education session on how to get their loved one to the intervention and I am always fascinated in terms of the unique ideas that are formed. Most of the time someone on the intervention team actually plans to drive their loved one to the intervention. A very important component in the afternoon of the education session is the planning for the consequences in case their loved one refuses help the day of the actual intervention. Each member of the team must look at their own enabling, be willing to stop or slow down their actions that assist their loved one continue to do their drug. Then look at specific enabling behaviors and state clearly they will stop that action immediately if their loved one refuses the help offered at the actual intervention. Examples include: A wife following through with a legal separation; a father refusing to shelter his son; brother not allowing him to see his nieces or nephews, unless he starts and continues treatment. We don't always have to state the consequences at the intervention, but if the person is refusing help we may have to employ them.

The first part of the pre-rehearsal includes practicing how to open the door and how to get their loved one to sit down where all the other members of the team are present. This can take at least 20 minutes. I always go early to decide what part of the house, apartment, church, temple, office etc is good for the intervention. I plan in advance who will sit where and I ask the team to bring photos of the past, loving events to be placed on the table set before their loved one. I have received and read the entire extra letters of those who could not participate for the educational session and have planned who will read them and in what sequence.

I ask the team after they have seated for the rehearsal on how they feel about where they have been placed by me. I listen to their comments and sometimes we change seating arrangements. They know their alcoholic/addict and I listen. I prepare, guide and trouble shoot them for the intervention, but they actually do the intervention. I learn with every family and every intervention.

We practice as if their loved one sat down and everyone reads their loved letters as well as practicing the consequences. The next day—the day of the intervention we rehearse one more time and we have at least one half hour to rest and eat something before it is expected that the loved one will be arriving. An actual intervention in my experience can be as short as 20 minutes or as long as 5 hours. Once the intervention is done a sense of relief and happiness is usually expressed by the team if their loved one says yes to recovery and desires to attend the treatment facility recommended by the team. Remorse, compliance and gratitude or anger and defiance to continue their drug of choice is expressed by their loved one. If defiance occurs for a long time determined by the interventionist then the consequences are given to their loved one by the family members. If their loved one agrees to get help they immediately transport their loved one to the facility after much hugs of joy. If the loved one refuse, the family must follow through on the consequences in a loving manner.

A closure session is one with the remaining team to find out what it was like for them and what they are going to do next. Most people are emotionally and physically drained. Then in 2 months and again in 6 months it is encouraged that we have follow up sessions that include their recovering loved one. Of course I take telephone calls from everyone as much as I am able to after the process and for the next 6 months. The alcoholic/addict is included in all the conversations since the seeds for a healthy family has been planted. It is not them against him/her. It is all of us against chemical dependency. I inquire about attendance at 12 step programs for everyone as well as counseling.

Many times I hear the alcoholic/addict is in strong recovery or relapsed and needs assistance again. Fewer times I hear the team continuing in a 12 step program and counseling. This saddens me, but I am only responsible for the effort and not the outcome (slogan in the 12 step program). Other times another alcoholic/addict in the family needs to be addressed and I help that family again.

I have been invited to one year anniversaries of the alcoholic/addict and I have seen members of the team active in 12 step meetings so I know recovery is continuing in that family.

Interventions are the first big step towards ongoing recovery for everyone in the family. I hear so many times, "I don't have the time to do an intervention." Well there is a saying in the 12 step meetings, "If you do what you always have done you will get what you always have gotten".

Do Interventions Really Work?

The first criteria to define success after an intervention is that the family and friends are all on the same page about their understanding about the disease of Chemical Dependency and their own healing process that we begin. This simply means they have started Al-anon/Nar-anon or Families Anonymous if they are not the alcoholic/addict themselves. If they are the alcoholic/addict to continue Alcoholics Anonymous or Narcotics Anonymous. Also, for many family members and friends counseling for their own issues surrounding this deadly disease might need to be addressed further by a professional licensed certified social worker, psychologist, or psychiatrist, all who specialize in the field of Chemical Dependency.

Another criteria of success is that the alcoholic/addict has admitted to needing help and is continuing to receive treatment and attending their respective 12 step meetings.

Everyone is asked to read their own 12 step literature, retain their own 12 step sponsor, and continue counseling until they no longer necessary. The counseling ends, and can resume later again, but the 12 step involvement lasts a lifetime.

You see the alcoholic/addict and the family members travel similar paths through healing. Both require self help group involvement on a maintenance level for the rest of their lives. Secondly, both alcoholic and family/friends may need therapy to continue what has been started during the intervention. The results I have witnessed and that have been given to me about actual post interventions are as follows:

I have been asked many times to attend a loved one's first anniversary in Alcoholics Anonymous along with the family. It is always a moving experience for me to hear and see the results of sobriety and abstinence for one year. If I am lucky enough to be at the family table watching their loved one speak with perhaps a little child holding on to me or another family member sitting close by it seems we are having tears of joy and love for the miracle that we are experiencing. I tell you that this is the next best feeling for me besides listening to their loved one state on the day of the intervention that they want the help that is being offered. The satisfaction of my job is indescribable.

I might be walking in my neighborhood and a sister of a loved one might see me and state," Do you remember you did an intervention on my younger brother? He is living in Florida and is attending AA meetings regularly and has an excellent job." What a feeling of joy in my heart.

I am exercising at a local gym and a mom asks me, "Do you remember my son and what happened at our intervention? Well, he is sober and working in Manhattan and has a solid future. Thank you so much for helping him get back his life and for getting my life back as well. I have lost 30 lbs, attend self help groups and feel great."

A thank you note stated, "Thank you Eileen for getting us to go where we needed to go. Words have not been invented to fully express our gratitude and appreciation for saving our daughter. We shall never forget the intervention. You told us how to proceed and it was the most beautiful and unforgettable experience. God Bless and keep you and the wonderful job you do."

Healing Process Of The Family During The Education

My experience has been that once the family accepts the disease concept of chemical dependency and begins to look at the family disease it opens the door to their enabling. Enabling is doing anything for the alcoholic/addict that they can do for themselves. Well it is amazing after several rehabilitations and outpatient counseling stints by the alcoholic/addict the family somehow sometimes never goes to the family weekend, family day or meet with the outpatient facility treating their loved one. They hear vaguely about Al-anon/Nar-anon and Families Anonymous. They like the alcoholic/addict don't accept their disease and refuse to start their healing. They are always looking on how to control their addict, yet the same things are being asked of them and they do the exact same thing like before the intervention. They ignore the knowledge given to them and do exactly what they have always done so they get what they have always gotten. During the education session part of the intervention the key is the entire family is asked to surrender and accept.

Therefore, each individual must look at their physical, emotionally, mental and spiritual deterioration. They must look at how their constant obsession about their addict allows them to ignore all others including themselves. They begin to understand the living and breathing their alcoholic/addict can't control their alcoholic/addict, yet they thought it could sometimes. Now just like the alcoholic/addict learns in treatment their priority must be step one: We are powerless over alcohol/drugs and our lives have become unmanageable. The family/friends learn step one: We are powerless over the alcoholic/addict and our lives have become unmanageable. Once everyone accepts unmanageability they begin to address the beginning of their recovery.

These are some examples of enabling:

1. A father still gives money to his married adult addicted daughter with three children and she uses it to buy cocaine. He has been giving it to his daughter without his son-in-law's knowledge. He knew it was wrong, but he felt guilty for his parenting of this particular daughter.

2. An aunt is knowledgeable about her sister's daily drinking while taking care of her three nieces. The brother-in-law is deceased. The aunt gives up trying to get help for her sister. She never gives consequences to her sister and never calls child protective services until I hear as an interventionist about this dire situation. I start an intervention ASAP and get adult supervision for those children immediately. One of the consequences for the intervention will be if she refuses help for her chemical dependency her children will be taken away from her.

3. A father and mother are both giving a grown son free room and board, paying for his car etc. Also, they give him money to drink and drug. They feel sorry for him and don't know what else to do for years.

4. A girlfriend is paying for rent, food and mounting bills by working 2 jobs while her live in drug addicted boyfriend goes on the internet and buys all the drugs he wants. Meanwhile, his mother delivers breakfast and his girlfriend makes dinner for him every night. These are actual events!

How could this be occurring? You see as a family member they don't focus on what they are doing, they just focus on what their alcoholic/addict is not doing or doing. Once the family admits to their own behavior and clearly see the futile uselessness of their behavior they become willing to change. Sometimes they change during the process of an intervention and resort back to the secrecy toward each other and go back to enabling. Other times the family has no more secrets, but they are not perfect. Many family members stop their enabling slowly.

The action of taking care of their alcoholic/addict is profoundly devastating. Many families members are physically worn either emaciated or overeating, they experience insomnia, or sleep all day long. They have many sick days due to arguments the night before with their alcoholic/addict just as the alcoholic/addict has many sick days due to hangovers. The family members experience physical and verbal abuse from their alcoholics/addicts and visa versa. The viscous cycle feeding off each other and then the rest of the family/friends off each other brings about the main core of the disease of chemical dependency. Everyone is concerned about the alcoholic/addict impending death, jail time etc. Yet some of the family members may have considered suicide themselves or have done something to save their addict that jail time could be in the cards for them as well.

Family Healing

"We must look at ourselves instead of pointing fingers at the addict. (This is from the "Courage to Change" book in Al-anon.) The family also admits to other behaviors not even associated with their addict and special counseling may be necessary. Family Wellness is the basic foundation for the family recovery. The family is taught to look at what are the good things happening in their family. Perhaps a new grandchild was born. Is someone recognizing this? What are the wonderful small everyday things that are going on? What the interventionist is accomplishing is that their focus is off the alcoholic/addict and on the good things in themselves individually in each family member/friend. The family usually reacts with relief and understands the importance of wellness. They also begin to understand if the family is more positive and focusing on healthier behaviors the alcoholic/addict will look forward to joining this healthy family. During the intervention process each family member and friend ask their loved one to join them in recovery. It is not saying the alcoholic/addict is bad or that their behavior is bad.

They are just saying we have started our healing and we are moving forward in a 12 step way of life. Please join us in recovery so we can all follow a 12 step way of life. If this really happens the chain of chemical dependency is weakening.

What Happens When
The Intervention Is Over?

If we are successful and the loved one agrees to enter treatment and the family agrees to enter their treatment the key is to continue for everyone involved.

The closure session is usually upbeat with happiness and some joy as well as some fear when the alcoholic/addict comes home. Sometimes at the closure session other alcoholics/addicts are identified and treated while other unique situations occur that need specialized referrals. Follow up by the interventionist with the family members and their loved one within three to six months is crucial on how successful this intervention was. First, the loved one may still be clean and sober. If not, how to reinstate treatment and stress the importance of the 12 step meetings. Perhaps there is a co-occurring disorder that needs diagnosis or a dual diagnosis treatment appears to be needed. As an interventionist I must be open-minded and always kept abreast of cutting edge treatment such as some other types of relapse prevention. Secondly, is the family continuing 12 step meetings and maybe they may need more intensive even perhaps inpatient co-dependency treatment for their family disease of chemical dependency. Whoever is not in healthy recovery during those crucial six months post the intervention needs to be referred

It is unbelievable how many times I have heard either that the alcoholic/addict has stopped 12 step meetings and they have gone back to their drug of choice and the family/friends have stopped 12 step meetings and gone back to their drug of choice, their loved one.

Wellness in the alcoholic/addict and the family members/friends begins when they take care of their own physical bodies, begin to look at their own emotional, spiritual, and psychological state. Each individual begins to enjoy life and get through the rough spots without blaming others for their problem.

They look at themselves and decide how to act with much consultation with their sponsor, home group, and their higher power.

Over the years I have been privileged to see and hear the results of recovery for the whole family. Recovery is alive and strong in the world. Those of you who haven't witnessed recovery and who might be understandably skeptical might ask, "How do you believe there is hope to reduce and prevent chemical dependency?" Start with an intervention assessment with a reputable interventionist. Start with an appropriate self help group and become open-minded and surround yourself with recovering people. Your attitude will change and your load in life will become lighter and the day to day activities will appear somehow easier. If you don't want the latter you can return to your misery.

Telephone thank you calls examples are the following"

1. Thank you and God Bless you. My daughter has completed inpatient treatment and is attending daily AA meetings. She is 22 years old and even when there was ice and snow on the street I said, "Are you sure you want to go to an AA meeting tonight?" She answered, "Mom, when I was getting high it snowed like this and I coped dope and drank I can certainly go to a meeting clean and sober. I just might choose a closer meeting." What recovery!

2. "My wife completed inpatient treatment and is attending AA meetings. I have made the order of protection permanent and she knows I mean business. She is clean even though some days she is in a foul mood. Other times it feels like I have my family back. It is a great feeling. I am attending Al-anon meetings and I am the refreshment person in my home group. My men's Al-anon meeting is a lifesaver. Thank you."

3. "My son is 6 months sober after four rehabilitations and countless outpatient programs. It is a true miracle. He is now getting opportunities to paint for people who will actually help him pay for his bills. His sponsor is over everyday and he goes to meetings and really breathes the AA program."

4. "I am sober 2 years now. I have a great relationship with my son and I am now not afraid of retirement someday. My AA meetings are always primary and I finally accept who I am, a recovering alcoholic and it is great!"

5. "Here I am the attorney that was the bum on the street with dishelved hair and smelly clothes. Now I am clean and sober and now a practicing attorney again. My sobriety is first and everything else follows good,

bad, or something in between. My higher power and my sponsor help me every step of the way. Life is great!"

6. "Please come to my first anniversary in AA. You know you saved my life and I have my wife back, but most importantly I have a life instead of a dark dingy basement with empty beer cans."

7. An 82 year old man thanks me for his adult children giving him tough love. Today he is allowed to visit his grandchildren because he is clean and sober. In sobriety he has found a purpose in life and that is to give wisdom to his grandchildren.

8. "My son relapsed and is living in a crack house. His wife and children have left him, but he is now willing to go back to recovery again. Thank God. I have been attending Al-anon and doing a lot of praying."

9. "My daughter died six months ago due to an overdose of alcohol at a party. I want to help other children not go down that path of alcohol poisoning. I belong to Families Anonymous, but I want to do more so I can remember my daughter's life. Can you help me?"

10. "My husband goes to meetings all the time and he is active in AA service. I am involved in Al-anon, but I am afraid for my children. I know I can't control them. Please help."

Families have all kinds of intergenerational addictions. When the alcoholic/addict starts recovery(attending self help meetings and remaining chemical free including alcohol and marijuana, etc)Families can possibly experience the following which has been adapted from the Roots and Wings program on page 11 in the parent manual printed by Hazelden.

Honest,clear communication with one another
Strong individual spiritual base and strong family spiritual base
Caring about other people and also caring and taking care of one's own self

The slogan from Alcoholics Anonymous and Al-anon such as EASY DOES IT, FIRST THINGS FIRST, ONE DAY AT A TIME, LIVE AND LET LIVE, AND LET GO AND LET GOD are state to oneself and to others and acted upon daily.

The 12 steps are worked on a daily basis.
The 12 traditions are also worked on daily.
Experience, strength and hope are given and received.

There is tremendous hope for the family recovery when the newly sober/ clean alcoholic/addict finally gets continuous sobriety and other alcoholics/ addicts are identified via interventions or willingly go to help themselves. Some alcoholics/addicts get worse and end up severely psychiatrically damaged, in jail or dead. The family mourns and now looks for survival for the entire family. They attend 12 step meetings(looking at the 12 steps in depth) in order to change their attitudes and learn how to support themselves and each other. Love replaces hatred. Forgiveness replaces resentment. Clear communication replaces manipulation. Laughter replaces violence.

Anyone can experience recovery in the alcoholic/addict at an open AA/Na meeting and recovery in the family members at an open Al-anon/Al-ateen meeting. You can attend an Al-anon anniversary in which the members celebrate how long the Al-anon group has been in existence compared to AA/NA anniversaries in which they celebrate the individual's own recovery. At an Al-anon anniversary there may be an AA speaker, an Al-anon speaker and an Al-ateen speaker. Each person will tell their experience strength and hope by explaining how the 12 steps/slogans etc have assisted in their lives. There may be food, as well as music and dancing afterward. The key ingredient is to show the public how AA/NA, Al-anon/Al-atteen works.

At an AA/NA anniversary they usually have a person speaking for them and also the person celebrating how many years in the program also speaks about how the meetings have assisted them staying clean and sober.

They are all finding themselves and find happiness at times and are beginning to understand alcoholism and drug addiction in their family. The stories told about their lives are awe inspiring. It is especially poignant in that of an Al-ateen speaker in which the teenager recounts the ravages of the family disease of chemical dependency and then tells us about their recovery work in the 12 step work in Al-ateen. Sometimes they make you cry and then laugh. The experience is hard to describe unless you are there in person.

Another special group in Al-anon is called Al-anon AC(Adult Child). When they speak about recovery they could describe their own path to healthy from growing up in a family filled with addiction or they themselves are alcoholics/addicts in recovery who are now delving into the family disease they experienced as children and young adults.

Why Not?

On average families wait about 15 to 20 years before doing an intervention. They wonder, "Maybe he /she is not that bad to warrant such a drastic action. I will try to convince you to call and make an appointment with an interventionist in order to possibly save your alcoholic/addict's life. Yes, I know it isn't easy. Write down what specific situation caused by the family member's drinking/drugging is finally unacceptable to you.

Most of the time family members/friends consider an intervention in which the alcoholic/addict is in the final stages of addiction. I have done may interventions in which the alcoholic/addict is severely emaciated and appears ready for the grave or have "Wet Brain" and go directly into a long stay at the hospital or end up in a nursing home. This is waiting too long.

The decision if and when to do an intervention is all up to you. It would be nice to reach alcoholics/addicts in the first and second stages of chemical dependency before body rot sets in as described by Dr. Ohm's as the major symptom of the third stage of addiction.

Some people make the decision of starting an intervention because, "Our brother is daily driving to work drunk." "My wife is driving the kids to baseball high." "My husband lost his job and our house is teetering on foreclosure." "My wife, an attorney is giving our children baths drunk."

What is the situation for you? If you are at your final straw, the next action is to call a professional interventionist and keep the children and society safe by taking the appropriate action in that regard. The most important part is if your family/friends are ready to give their all to save the alcoholic/addict's life and the lives of everyone else in contact with the addicted person. An experienced interventionist can help you decide if an intervention is necessary and possible in your situation. During the intervention assessment a determination will be make in terms of which type of intervention should be utilized and who should be involved. Also, treatment facilities for the involved will be recommended in terms of the best fit for the individual and their treatment needs. This assessment usually takes 1 ½ hours in which the team involved will be explored. There should be no pressure from anyone to move forward. After this session in which two family/friends take part in, they will discuss in private if this is what they really want for their loved one. You may stop at this point if you or your interventionist feels you are not ready. In that case it is discussed what is necessary to be accomplished before all involved more forward. An example for pausing might be your family needs to get stronger emotionally. Some examples of pausing are:

1. I have heard the story of a 40 year old son who sleeps all day long and does cocaine all night. His parents give him money for the cocaine because he has threatened them that if they don't he will kill them. These particular parents have borrowed so much money that they are in danger of losing their primary residence. The issue of safety for the parents, counseling and Al-anon needs to commence before we might consider a scaled down intervention called a Heart to Heart or a Systemic intervention instead of a full blown Johnson Model type of intervention.

2. A divorced daughter does drugs daily and her children are watched by the grandparents every day. The grandparents and grandchildren watch this young woman destroy herself before their eyes. We need to safeguard the people involved while we move forward on an intervention.

3. A son is jailed again, a daughter-in-law is ingesting drugs and the grandchildren are drinking heavily. The grandparents of these grandchildren feel afraid, overwhelmed and helpless. Safety for all involved is a priority and steps must be taken before an intervention must be considered.

4. A husband who is a successful engineer and is heavily drinking despite severe liver damage at 42 years old. He recently was treated for a heart attack, but still puts on the outer appearance of a good husband and father. He may be a good husband and father, but he has become so sick from the disease of chemical dependency. His wife and children are now afraid the most important man in their lives may die.

How does anyone of these families or your family decide to change. Simply by calling a reputable interventionist and start the process of a chemical dependency family intervention. Some of the examples waited too long. Others need immediate attention to certain situation and then the intervention can commence. How severe do your consequences have to be in order to make that call for help? Maybe you feel you have done everything except an intervention so all you can accomplish is damage control to a new set of consequences ahead. This is an erroneous thought because the consequences do become more severe with or without your control called enabling. The end results can be death for the alcoholic/addict as well as death for the family/friends. Psychiatric hospitalizations for the alcoholic/addict and their family/friends is definitely possible. Along with that can come multiple rehabilitations for the alcoholic/addict, multiple outpatient treatments for both the alcoholics/addicts and their family/friends. Another possibility is no treatment for all concerned and the progression of the disease continues. Only the alcoholic/addict and the family/friends surrendering and accepting their disease will result in recovery for everyone who is willing to work on their own individual recovery. Don't forget the alcoholic/addict is addicted to their chemical and the family/friends are addicted to their alcoholic/addict. You see chemical dependency causes individual and family demise unless change occurs. Sometimes chemical dependency skips a generation and sometimes one generation gets the whole family disease in that specific generation.

An example of such a devastation is the family of two sisters. Their mom is a recovering alcoholic and attending AA meetings regularly. Unfortunately, her oldest daughter died due to a drug overdose and left her two children and husband behind. Those children have major eating disorders and severe conduct disorders. The other sister is alive, but married a violent alcoholic with bipolar disorder and this woman's two sons have bipolar disorder and attention deficit disorder.

Of your family is devastated please start the process of recovery or if your family is starting down the road of devastation start recovery early.

Why Wait?

When you have experienced the situation that was in your perspective overboard, START RECOVERY ASAP. What are some of the obstacles?

Time: "I don't know if I can get all these people together or to write letter." Well interventions can be done during the week or weekends. If done on a weekend it could be started on a Friday night from 7pm to 10pm. Then continued on Saturday from 10 am until the afternoon. Then on Sunday from the am until sometime at the end of that day or sooner.

Money: "I don't have enough money." Sometimes scholarships may be available. Interventionist charge $3000.00 up to $25,000.00 for the intervention. This does not include for some transportation, hotel accommodations etc. In terms of treatment Medicaid is available, private insurance may pay for parts of treatment, and finally there must be the thought to private self pay. I have stated to families that a funeral may cost as much as $14,000.00, so instead of paying for a funeral pay for an intervention and treatment. Also, here in the northeast home values have gone up so I tell families to consider getting home equity loans to pay for treatment. On the other hand, if families have been dried up by their loved one who is disable by this disease or refer them to detoxification/rehabilitations that will automatically apply for government assistance for their loved one.

When?

When to start an intervention is dependent on how healthy the family/friends, alcoholics/addicts are at the time of the intervention assessment. The suggestion would be as soon as humanly possible after the above have been considered.

What Particular Situation Makes It Concrete In The Minds Of The Family That An Intervention Is Warranted?

The alcoholic/addict is doing their thing—everything is about the next drink/drug from the time they wake up to the time they go to sleep if they go to sleep. This condition becomes progressively worse; therefore, the family/friends begin to feel progressively worse about their feelings of abandonment, lack of companionship and no sex life. Later the family and friends fear psychiatric hospital stays, jail time or death for their family member. If the alcoholic/addict is a child the family feels desperate also feeling the child's death, psychiatric hospital stay or jail time. How bad is bad before it is time to start the process of an intervention? For everyone it differs. Some examples are:

1. "My elderly father fell down the stairs and cut his face badly and hurt his foot while he was intoxicated."
2. "My husband drives home drunk every night."
3. "My wife nearly drowned one of our kids last night when she was bathing them while she was high."
4. "My brother drinks out of control once in a while, but he is causing trouble now. During his last cab ride home he threw up all over the cab after leaving the conference room of his corporate building."
5. "My daddy gets drunk every night and passes out on the kitchen floor."
6. "My mommy is drunk while driving my brother and I to our soccer games."
7. "My aunt dresses in a disheveled manner and slurs her speech and smells of alcohol every time we see her."

8. "My lover verbally abuses me constantly every night after he has been drinking."
9. "My girlfriend gets drunk every night making dinner and I am alone for the rest of the night."
10. "My cousin is roaming the streets and drinking meanwhile he has a nice condominium to live in."
11. "My co-worker is always high and since we are friends I keep on covering for him, but I can't cover for him anymore."

When is it the right time to say "WE NEED HELP WE NEED AN INTERVENTION."

Fear

Are you afraid you or your alcoholic/addict will die? Fear of the alcoholic/addict going to jail, fear of another DWI arrest, fear of you alcoholic/addict killing someone by a car accident while they are driving drunk, fear of your alcoholic/addict accidentally injuring or killing their children, fear of your alcoholic/addict losing control verbally or physically against other family/friends, fear of them getting fired, etc.

Why Do So Many People Wait So Long To Get Their Alcoholic/Addict Help?

Sometimes an intervention is not needed to get your alcoholic/addict help. I am surprised to find out how many people never even approach their loved one about their disease and ask them if the want help. The key is to know ahead to time the help you are offering and be ready to give them the information when they say yes. Please by all means get that person the help they ask for within your means. Even if your loved one gets help is essential that the family receive an education about the family disease and start getting help because remember this is a family disease. It is important that you have researched treatment with a treatment professional in order to fit the needs of your particular loved one.

Scenario

Your alcoholic/addict states, "I want to go for help." You can answer with, "Here it is. You can call and make arrangements now." Even if your family member enters treatment without an intervention Yes You must go for help yourself. If he or she does well in treatment or fails at that time you must continue your 12 step program and specific treatment for the entire family.

I feel overwhelmed sometimes by the emotional pain of these families and pray for them and all families struck by the disease of chemical dependency.

The above cases are extreme, but if the disease goes on unchecked this may happen in the future generations in your family. I am not saying it still can't happen, but to do nothing at all just seem to me not an option. There is always hope if there is one or many nonrecovering alcoholics/addicts in your family. Please give an intervention a real concerted effort. If your alcoholic/addict goes back to their old patterns of behavior you know you have tried everything. Also, you have started the prevention process in the rest of your family and friends.

Does Prevention Really Work?

I have learned that protective factors such as high expectations from family, school and community and self as well act as a strong support. Problem solving skills, empathy, good communication, a sense of humor, a sense of purpose, meaningful participation in our world, positive self esteem and independence are all important protective factors.(Adapted from the Roots and Wings parenting program printed by Hazelden)

The most important key prevention ingredient is believing in alcohol abstinence and of course illegal drug abstinence for our children is paramount. For young adults over 21 years old and no family history of chemical dependency responsible drinking is two drinks for a man and one drink for a woman in one day. Of course the person driving will not drink any amount of alcohol and of course no illegal drugs under any circumstances.

I know our children experiment, but how the family responds to these situations are crucial. Furthermore, How the community supports the parents is the foundation of the prevention of drugs and alcohol in our youth.

You may wonder what it takes to really go through the process of an intervention. It takes:

COURAGE

Courage emerges when children who were originally filled with fear, confront their addicted parents and are supported by their aunt, uncles, and cousins. The family promises to take care of them while their parents are receiving chemical dependency treatment.

Help creeps through when elderly parents of an adult drug addicted son understand their enabling and begin to change and plan to continue to eliminate all their enabling. Therefore, they open the door of hope for their son.

LOVE

Love is where each family member can't even remember if or when they felt love for this addict, they are intervening on. Of course, there are some warm feelings, but anger and resentment have clouded them. They state, "Eileen we have no memories of love." While going through the education with their higher power power's help the love emerges. Love is the most powerful feeling in the world. I have witnessed during an intervention a father who was never demonstrative to his addicted son place his hand on his son's knee and through tears he tells his son for the first time how much he loves him. The son's eyes welled up. That was the first part of success for that particular intervention.

A GROWING FAITH

A growing faith occurred when an adult child of an alcoholic father had faith that his father would desire to continue to be in his grandchildren's lives. The stipulation would be that his father would start and continue sobriety. This would give his father the possibility to have a continued and improved relationship with his grandchildren.

FORGIVENESS

Forgiveness occurs perhaps when a wife realizes that the alcoholic husband had been having affairs with alcoholic women under the influence of his addiction. His values of fidelity may return and he may become faithful again, if sobriety is reached. It is possible by her gaining the clear understanding of the disease of chemical dependency, that she may begin to forgive him and there is hope for her marriage after he starts recovery.

PERSISTENCE

Persistence occurs many times when parents of a teenage alcoholic/addict are tired of being persistent in their parenting. They don't know if they can emotionally go through with the intervention process, yet they somehow regain some energy to take the action necessary.

The most important part is the family/friends must be ready to give their ALL to save the alcoholic/addict's life during and after the intervention one day at a time. The purpose of this book is to catalyze you to talk to your family/friends and make the telephone call for a possible intervention if all else has failed.

What If The Intervention Does Not Work?

If your alcoholic/addict continues to drink/drug after the treatment that has been given to them you know you have tried everything and now can walk away without guilt. It is important to note that new treatments are being done with excellent results so it is imperative to keep abreast of the newest techniques to treat relapse. You can be the information pipeline if your alcoholic/addict desires more help, but you must stop begging him to try. He/She must be willing themselves to look at their relapsing after the intervention is completed.

First, you and the rest of the family have started your own recovery from the family disease of chemical dependency and maybe your alcoholic/addict may decide recovery later by themselves. They will always be invited into the recovering family as long as they are working on their own recovery, but if they choose not to stop their addictive behavior the family moves on and encourages healthy behaviors in the rest of the family.

Another concern is what about if I don't like my newly sober alcoholic/addict? Well it is one day at a time framework, in which you both learn the newness in both of you and begin a new recovery relationship together.

Case Histories

CASE ONE

A husband arrived during my lunch and started to bring empty bottles of wine in my office. When I returned my office smelled of old wine and a man stood waiting to see me. He said, "I brought all the bottles that I found in my basement to show you how much my wife consumes and to see if my wife is an alcoholic." He came in desperation and was worried about the safety of his children even though he had known about his wife's drinking for years. It had become a crisis for him because his business had slowed down and he was able to witness first hand how his wife's drinking behaviors were affecting their children. After we started talking he appeared adamant that their children had no idea of their mother's drinking. Yet I persistently explained how the children knew more than adults would admit to themselves. This is called denial. Also, I explained how children are very effective many times breaking through the parent's denial of the drinking than adults are. Finally he relented and was willing to have the children meet with me and some of them would be a part of the intervention. Of course, I followed with all the intervention assessment protocol. This book is not for the professional to learn how to do an intervention, but to educate the families out there who needs an intervention. So, I will not discuss this case as a review for professionals, rather to help families understand how difficult yet successful interventions can be.

The day of this particular intervention arrangements were make for a full time temporary nanny to car for the children for the entire process leading up to the intervention and afterwards. The father began attending Al-anon meetings and he brought his oldest son to Al-ateen and therapy prior to the intervention. The intervention was delayed until I felt the family was ready.

The education was attended by Barr(husband), George(ten year old son), Henry (8 year old child), Loretta and Sam(wife's parents), Joe and

Anne(husband's parents),Harriet and Jean(wife's sisters). ALL NAMES ARE FICTICOUS

The children offered insight to the family in terms of the severity of their mom's drinking and offered the punch line to break through their mother's denial of her drinking. During the intervention George state, "Dad is such a wimp and he never wants to go on the rides with me. Remember two years ago when we went to Disney World and we went on Space Mountain together. We laughed and when we got off the ride you tickled me and I thought you were the best mother in the world. But last week when you drove me to my soccer game with my little brother in the back seat and a bottle of vodka in a brown paper bag in the back seat of the car I cried. My coach came over and asked me what was wrong and I just kept on crying and then my teammates cam over and I said nothing. Mom, I was afraid that you would kill by baby brother and yourself drinking and driving like that." "Where do you want me to go?" asked his mother. He replied, "I want you to go to the place Daddy found to help you. She replied, "I will go." Since then the children are being driven by their grandparents or nanny while their father is working.

The mom went into rehabilitation, but unfortunately she had relapsed numerous times and attended numerous rehabilitations and halfway houses. It has been five years and she is still drinking. Her husband has divorced her and attends Al-anon and the children attend Al-ateen. The children hope and pray for their mom's recovery. Hopefully the risk of chemical dependency will be reduces in this woman's children and grandchildren. There is still hope for her as well. Maybe one day I may get a call from her stating she is in strong recovery and rekindling her relationship with her children. This is a success story because some family members are in recovery. Hopefully more will follow in the future.

CASE TWO

A mom and day came in for an intervention assessment for their son Arthur 21 years old. He lives out of state, drinks alcohol and smokes marijuana daily. He started using both of those chemicals when he was 14 years old without his parent's knowledge. They felt he had self esteem issues, social anxiety, and was diagnosed with attention deficit disorder when he was 14. Arthur recently stopped marijuana so he could breath easier with his outdoor activities. He told his parents he had recently developed asthma. He happened to be going to court for his first DWI that Monday and this was the Friday before. I tried to get an evaluation completed so that the court might recommend treatment, but the family was unable to do so due to the length of distance between them and their son. Therefore, a referral was made so the son could have an evaluation done and hopefully receive treatment. So, an intervention was not necessary as long as the young man was willing to follow through on the recommendation of the referring provider.

You see a person may come in for an intervention and it may not be necessary all the time.

CASE THREE

An intervention was planned with Cecilia and Dab(mother and father), Amanda and Michael(sister and brother), Jeffrey(uncle in AA), Carol and Pat(aunts), Ron(son's former teacher) Jerome came from a wealthy family, was an avid skier, and a musician who dropped out of college due to his drinking/drugging. Because of the intervention he went into recovery and is still attending AA/NA meetings. He has a sponsor in both programs and does service in both. Presently, he is working in a restaurant. His entire family attends Al-anon and for those addicted to chemicals they are attending their respective programs. The family is in recovery and that is a success story.

CASE FOUR

During an intervention assessment a son who is a practicing medical doctor spoke about his alcoholic mom who was 58 years old. She had major medical symptoms of advanced stages of chemical dependency. Mary exhibited abdomen distention, jaundice, and was drinking daily. The education included the following people: (just like all the other cases all the names are ficticous.

Henry(husband and medical doctor as well), Jonathon, Robert, James(sons who were all medical doctors), Lisa(aunt), Ann(maternal mother). During the intervention mom listened to her family intently and entered a medical hospital for detoxification and alcohol rehabilitation and today she is in strong recovery in AA and remaining clean and sober, reading her AA literature, and doing service in AA. Her family of medical doctors now educate their parents and refer their alcoholics/addict to help and give the correct information to the family members of alcoholics/addicts in their medical practices.

CASE FIVE

A mother and sister arrived to discuss about a son/brother Harold(only 110 lbs). He is emaciated, homeless, and drinking daily. The education included:

Helen (mom), Angela(sister), Ed(uncle), Emily(aunt), Jean(godmother), Eugene(friend).The names again are ficticious.

The family was well prepared and Harold willingly without hesitation took the help being offered. He was so sick he thought I was a family member and thanked me and called me aunt. He was admitted into a hospital for three weeks instead of three to five days for detoxification due to his medical condition. Later her attended longer term rehabilitation and still lives in a halfway house today. He has strong recovery and has gained weight and is participating family member that is gainfully employed.

CASE SIX

At the intervention assessment a sister and her husband spoke about her brother Hank and his cocaine addiction. During the education process Diana(sister, Tony(brother-in-law), Steve(nephew), Kathleen and Michael(mother and father), Joe(brother) brought about an unusual occurrence during our coffee break. The person we were intervening on's brother spoke to me privately and requested to be excused from the intervention. It was on the fact that if he spoke about his brother's cocaine in the presence of his family the brother involved may bring up the fact of this brother's affair. He was married and his wife just had their first child. As the interventionist, I had to work at the project at hand and asked his brother Joe in front of his family preparing for the intervention not to be involved in order to focus on the task of Hank's possible recovery. This particular couple entered counseling and Joe said the scare of being caught brought him to the realization of how dangerous this affair was to his marriage. He consented and started marriage counseling on his own. It is amazing how the intervention also helped Hank's brother. The family confronted their loved one and he willingly went into rehabilitation and is still clean today. Some of his family members still attend Al-anon while others have stopped their attendance of 12 step programs.

CASE SEVEN

A mother and son spoke about a son/sibling living at home with mom. He was not working, not attending school, doing drugs every night and sleeping all day. The education session was attended by June(mom), Jack(brother), Andrew and Sal(two friends from college who now work on Wall Street). In this situation, the people who convinced this loved one to go for help were his college buddies, who had developed careers and families. The loved one was surprised that they took time away from their employment to help him. This young man is almost finished with his Masters Degree in Education. He is clean and sober and attends Narcotics Anonymous meetings on a regular basis.

CASE EIGHT

A mother and son arrived and spoke about a daughter/sibling. Joanne was a 28 year old addicted to alcohol and cocaine. At the education session five sisters and the loved one's mother worked feverishly to learn and accept. Joanne went willingly into treatment at the intervention, but two days later the three daughters called to inform me that their mother, who was also an alcoholic unknown to me started drinking on a daily basis since the intervention. The family had hid this from me. So I did a mini intervention on their mother disguised as a closure session. Both family members practically at the same time went into treatment, while the rest of the family attended Al-anon meetings and counseling.

CASE NINE

This intervention started with a call from a daughter living in Arizona about her mother living on Long Island with her drug addicted son with whom she was enabling. He slept all day and went out almost every night to do drugs. The daughter was fearful for her mother's life. Her mother was in denial of how the disease of chemical dependency had taken her son into the final stages of addiction. She was a hostage in her own home. After many phone calls and sessions with the mother she finally agreed to start the intervention process. Of course, elder abuse was reported by the family and the interventionist.

The education included Jennifer(mom), Alison(sister), Maryellen(aunt), Howie(cousin), Eleanor(neighbor), and his pastor. The names are ficticious.

During the intervention the son refused help at first, but the daughter stayed at my request to support the mother until the son understood that his mother meant business. Meaning if her refused help his clothes were to be placed in black garbage bags in front of her home and the locks would be changed. She would not open the door for him. The son did leave the treatment facility after two days of being admitted. He went back home and to his surprise his sister and mother refused him access to his former home.

He, after many complaints, returned to the rehabilitation center and is in recovery today. The rest of the family hopefully is attending Al-anon.

CASE TEN

She was a 32 year old female with two children 8 and 7 years old. She had a cocaine addiction and her nasal septum was destroyed from continued use of the drug. She had entered five rehabilitation centers and still continued to use cocaine. Her husband complained she stole from their checking account and opened new credit card accounts in his name and borrowed money from her father and mother. The aunt, uncle, sister, husband father, and two friends attended the education. The problem was that the family's enabling, especially the father's was out of control. He unknowingly kept on fueling the addiction. Her father finally realized his rescuing and covering up for his daughter's behavior, was only backfiring. He surrendered to the idea that it was not the best way to deal with his guilt. As the education session progressed, the family had told me about another family member that had committed suicide while using drugs. This family portrayed dramatic sadness. The husband and children needed intense counseling as well as attendance in Al-anon and Al-atot(for younger children). The family needed to find babysitting arrangements initially and eventually a long term nanny or family member willing to care for the children. The family cleaned the house and took care of the children while their loved one entered rehabilitation. This family needed to help these children for an extended period of time, since their loved one needed long term rehabilitation as well as a halfway house.

Intervention is the key to assist families in their own disease. They must break through their denial in order to bring about the start of healing. Then gain the continuation with professional counseling. A 12 step way of life is the maintenance for the rest of the family's life. The hope in the above case is that the loved one comes home to a more loving environment with healthier family members. This brings about more protective factors against high risk relapse and a better chance of reduced incidence of the severity of the disease in the next generation.

What Does Long Term Recovery Look Like For The Alcoholic/Addict And For The Family/Friends?

Recovery in the alcoholic/addict comes when they realize they are not the center of the universe. They learn to live life without drinking/drugging. They achieve serenity sometimes and begin to deal with the ups and downs of everyday life with the continued support of their 12 step meetings, talking to their sponsor in the 12 step program, telling their story,(giving their experience, strength and hope), practicing the `12 steps in their lives, giving help to their sponsees, reading 12 step literature as well as performing other service in the 12 step program.

Recovery in the family/friends comes when they realize that they exist as a separate human being from their alcoholic/addict. They can live a detached life with love from their alcoholic/addict whether or not their alcoholic/addict is in recovery. They also achieve serenity sometimes and begin to deal with the ups and downs of life with the continued support of Al-anon, Nar-anon, Families Anonymous, etc. They attend their own 12 step meetings, talk to their sponsor in the 12 step program, give their experience, strength and hope, read 12 step literature, practice the 12 steps in their lives, give help to sponsees, as well ass other service work in their 12 step program.

As you see the alcoholic/addict vs. the family/friends follow a similar pattern of recovery. One is dealing with their addiction of the chemical and the other is dealing with the addiction of the alcoholic/addict. This is why the 12 steps apply to both.

To listen and really hear the experience, strength and hope of people in recovery even for those never afflicted with the family disease is truly an awe inspiring heart felt moment. Life defining moments are important building blocks for the formation of self. Recovery is strong and alive and I am here to testify that situation. The path from surrender that they can't go into recovery alone to acceptance into the recovery way of life is essential. Once there the people who accept it as a life time commitment are given the gift of the possibility of life time recovery. Recovery may include relapses in both programs. People pick themselves up, dust themselves off and start again. Others have continuous recovery in their 12 step program.

Of course, many alcoholics/addicts, family/friends need counseling for short or longer periods of time. Some have a multitude of co-occurring disorders that need special counseling. Other alcoholics/addicts are chronic relapsers and as treatment professional we are always searching for the newest techniques, etc to treat this brain disorder. Everyone should be open-minded to all the new and promising treatments on the horizon that can make major strides to jump start recovery or maintain recovery.

How Does Recovery Affect Future Generations Of A Family?

How about a father who is sober in AA and also attends Al-anon AC (Adult children of Alcoholics). His wife attends Al-anon and their son attends Al-ateen regularly. That is an example of a nuclear family in recovery. There are other examples of a wife in AA, her husband in Al-anon and their adult sons in Al-anon. I could go on and on. Recovery is out there and it is a beautiful thing.

How Does Recovery Affect The Family Generationally?

Well each person in recovery does affect positively those around them. One example is that a grandchild in kindergarten brought in the Big Book of AA for show and tell. The grandchild stated, "My grandpa goes to the AAAAAAAAAAAA's program. Out of the mouth of babes. If the next generation in your family witnesses recovery it does increase chances of early recovery in them. Meaning earlier identification of the active(person become alcoholic/addicted) disease of chemical dependency as well as the family disease. Also, it increases protective factors in which the premise is that abstinence from alcohol and other drugs in our family is clearly stated. Of course many people may need some type of psychotropic medication if there is a co-occurring disorder along with the diagnosis of chemical dependency. We can't control, but families can state their opinion in terms of the use of those chemicals our families have a predisposition to becoming addicted to. It surprises me that so many people in Al-anon who are not alcoholics/addicts seem to think they are immune of becoming addicted they are in a 12 step program for their family members. It is like playing Russian roulette with their lives. Most teenagers and young adults need limits and parents need to step up to the plate. Teachable moments is an easy concept that that has been advertised on TV as anti-drug messages.

Recovery in the next generation means that the parents, caregivers or guardians of children who are in recovery themselves pass on the gift to their children in their care. Each adult while working on their own recovery can pass down slogans, the 12 step approach, the anniversary celebrations and the literature to their offspring. Also, people can start prevention strategies with clear communication to their children. Using teachable moments helps parents talk to their children about all types of new and challenging situations. These discussions in turn, form a foundation for young people's values and their ability to solve problems, make decisions and live independently. The decision whether or not to use alcohol and other drugs is a personal one, but parents need to understand that their decision about chemical use and their ability to communicate expectations can and do influence their children. Using teachable moments helps parents clearly communicate their personal standards and expectations to their children(Roots and Wings Parenting Program from Hazelden).

I have been asked more than once by young recovering mothers who have young children, "Gee Eileen I am afraid for my children. I don't want them to go through what I have been through." We have heard that alcoholism runs in families. With new technologies and breakthroughs we are experiencing tremendous possibilities for multiple different researches with different treatment approaches. Yet we still can't control the chance of the disease erupting many times in one generation nor stop it in the future generations. What we can do is to be a good recovering adult role model by working the 12 steps in our lives. Also, stating clearly to our biological children with the history of addiction in their families to think about not drinking alcohol at all that is including those of you in Al-anon who think somehow you are immune to the active disease of chemical dependency.

We can educate our present and future generations and then LET GO AND LET GOD(slogan from the 12 step program). WE ARE RESONSIBLE FOR THE EFFORT AND NOT THE OUTCOME(another slogan from the 12 step program)

Furthermore, the choice of our children and grandchildren in terms of abuse and becoming addicted can be identified earlier and interventions can be done where needed. In the future my vision is that interventions will be commonplace. That it is a useful tool in order to gain earlier identification of the disease of chemical dependency, preferably in the first and second stages of the disease instead of the final stages. This in turn will affect whole communities. Hopefully community recovery will decrease the incidence of the disease of chemical dependency in our neighborhoods. Together we can make this happen, one intervention at a time one recovering family at a time.

Community Interventions

Many communities across the United States are now working together in order to reduce underage drinking and stop the use of illegal drugs in our youth. The clergy, business leaders, police departments, superintendents, principals, social workers, psychologists, nurses, parents, and students come together after they have completed a survey and begin to collectively attack the rampant ravages of underage drinking and drugging. I have had the pleasure to have two women with elementary school and junior high school children who were concerned with the alcohol and drug use in their community. These two women worked incessantly gathering information making contacts, gaining community support, and holding meetings with my advise. These two women started a systemic change to decrease young people consuming alcohol in their community. Another community task force was started by one woman who relentlessly pursued protective factors to prevent the increased likelihood of drugs and alcohol to young people. She like the two before her was sincerely dedicated with the highest ethical regard. These in a sense are community interventions. They confront parents living in their respective communities with the specific alcohol/drug problems with their children in their area. The community task force bombards the community with information in a realistic emotional way in order to break the denial of the community. Many times communities try to hide their problems because they are afraid their property values may fall if someone finds out or they are too ashamed to think it could be happening to their children or friend's children. Oh by the way this problem has nothing to do with shame. It has to do with a possibility of a brain disease developing in many young people in a community. Some communities really believe that they don't need prevention programs or just choose not to show up for education etc. lest someone talk about who showed up and maybe their family might be gossiped about in terms of having this problem. A lot of parents of teenagers believe it is "OK if their teenagers drink in their house, at least they can watch them and they are not driving." Others state, "As long as they don't get into trouble with the law or get physically sick I will look the other way when my teenager is drinking at unsupervised parties that I know about."

Lately, in my neck of the woods, prom activities and even if there should be proms are being questioned. One school even cancelled the prom altogether. Of course there was quite an uproar. Then hundreds of letter were sent to the school that cancelled the prom congratulating them for the courage to confront the denial of the problem of underage drinking.

It is not uncommon for some police departments in a local area to be inundated on weekends in the fall and winter and all week long in the spring and summer with drunk/high adolescents. We all know that some parents are out for the night/weekend and kids take advantage and have a drunk fest with as many as 50 plus kids in one house at one time. What is much more alarming is that parents are now having these drunken fests with kids of all ages in tow. Parents and kids sleep off their hangovers at friend's houses. It is happening. What about the kids in the park drinking/drugging and attacking police? What about when parents are called to the precinct because you Daniel is a regular there for drunkedness and there appears to neither consequences nor treatment being offered to young Daniel by his caregivers. (name ficticious). It is sad for me as a clinician. It is sad for the police, for the schools, for the hospitals, and for the communities. Where are we headed? Our youth, young adults and adults are being driven in higher numbers each day to chemical dependency. When is enough, enough? When are we going to stand up individual to individual, family to family, school to school, and neighborhood to neighborhood? Wake up in yourselves, your homes, your neighborhoods, schools, and your companies.

How Did It All Happen?

Today society is gradually destroying itself from within in terms of tolerating unacceptable behavior. Unacceptable behavior is becoming more prevalent and more bizarre. Many in the field of chemical dependency have been talking about families coming for help appear much more in crisis in the past few years.

Alcohol abuse is considered as heavy drinking and it is OK according to many mistaken people as long as you are not drinking and driving or not getting into trouble with the law. Binge drinking is looked upon as a badge of courage, a mountain to climb at college. Sometimes to perfect and master. Drinking in high school is looked upon by mistaken students as a rite of passage. Drinkinig in the middle school is viewed upon by the mistaken students as experimentation and a way to feel more grown up with the opposite sex.

Alcoholism is viewed by society as something bad or that the person is deformed. Society does not understand alcoholism as a disease that has the potential for prevention and sometimes can be identified person that needs treatment. Yet as it goes on undetected for some in middle school, for others in high school, and for others in college—society pretends it doesn't exist. In society's mind the only thing that exists is experimentation by adolescents and adults.

On TV numerous commercials has a remedy for society's problems or so called problems with a pill with lots of side effects. Don't get me wrong we need medication but sometimes that all you see on TV. The internet provides much erroneous information about alcohol/drugs. Drug dealers come from all backgrounds, all nationalities, and all socioeconomic backgrounds. There is no discrimination.

This means in order to intervene on the loved ones who are affected with alcohol and drug problems must be treated like any other patient with a chronic disease. Let me ask you—If know someone has diabetes and asks to buy them a chocolate bar do you go buy it especially if they pay you for it? Why ladies and gentlemen is this going on. First, they can get it themselves unless they are already debilitated from the disease of diabetes. Do you as individuals, families, schools and corporations encourage people with diabetes to eat sugary substances constantly? I think most people would say no.

Does The Family Understand That They Must Change?

When families understand that they must change and seek a different route even when their loved one seeks recovery, their loved one gets additional support towards their own long term recovery. If their loved one returns to drinking and drugging and the family has not changed all that has been done is relentless efforts in getting that person into recovery while not looking at their part in the family disease.

I listen to, "My son has entered four rehabilitation centers, two halfway houses, but never accepted the 12 step way of life." I ask since we last spoke last year have you attended 12 step meetings and counseling yourself? Their answer is usually, "I went to a few meetings and they were much worse than me or they wouldn't help me with my son." Yet how worse were they? The family member complains of constant insomnia, loosing their jobs, chest pains, increased blood pressure, their own marriage in trouble, etc. I tell them the 12 step meetings are to look at their behavior not the alcoholic/addict. So of course they are not focused on your loved one. Your loved one has their own 12 step meetings with their own sponsor, literature, group and counselor. There are plenty of people to help him and your are not needed as much.

Many times they are not listening. I guess the first part of my intervention is really a mini intervention on the people attending the intervention assessment especially if they are not open-minded to looking at themselves as pieces of the healthy puzzle. When I was a child or when I helped my children work puzzles I always did the four corners and worked inward. Not so successfully all the time, but that was my initial plan. In case of family members and friends not having the correct pieces or not willing to place the correct puzzle pieces together makes it quite difficult to complete the puzzle. I know when my children were small and we had an intricate puzzle it was placed on the dining room table. Some lost pieces were never found or we just couldn't complete it, but we could figure out most of it. I am not asking you to complete the puzzle of your family. I am only asking that the family is recognizable enough so that the alcoholic/addict can recognize the healthiness in his/her family.

We can have a greater degree of healthiness and each of us is responsible for our part. We can not point fingers at the alcoholic/addict. Each day we must look at the work we must do ourselves. If we can make ourselves better people our alcoholics/addicts can have role models. Everyone can change their actions and most importantly no one can blame anyone else.

Where I Come From?

My name originally was Eileen Mary Davis, first generation Irish Catholic. My deceased alcoholic father was a good, hard working church attending person. He drank alcohol daily way before I was born and until his death. My deceased mother was a hard working, church attending co-dependent until her death. She was a rageaholic, just reacting daily to my father's drinking. My father Edward Davis died as the result of alcoholism prematurely, but his death certificate stated the cause of death as pneumonia. My mother, Kathleen Davis at the time my husband and myself were attending my cousin's Patrick's eagle scout ceremony. My father decided to go to work and not attend. When the three of us returned home we found my father passed out by our brick steps and cement walk way that was covered with snow and ice. We proceeded with the help of neighbors to physically pick up my father, a 6 ft 2" 220 lb man up the stoop and into bed. At that time I was a practicing RN and I attended to his needs to deal with his hypothermia and frost bite. He was able to speak and wanted to be left alone until the morning. He awoke with fear because he desired to urinate and he was unable to walk. I called the ambulance and he was brought to the hospital. Until his death the family took care of him in the hospital. Since he was a patient in the hospital where I worked he got the best care from my co-workers and myself. Also, the rest of the family came daily to give him companionship and comfort. Why might you say? Well he was my Dad who would take me to my volunteer job at the hospital when I was a candystipper every Sunday by bus. His actions showed me he loved me although he never stated it to me.

Not one person mentioned the DT's he was experiencing while he was a patient during his first days at the hospital. Everyone denied he was going through withdrawal, including me because in those days in my house we just didn't talk about those things. He later experienced a hear attack that led to a come until his death. The hard part in the beginning was I never said good-bye to a man I adored despite all his flaws stemming from his alcoholism. My mother on the other hand, didn't want him to come back home, because she felt he would be another major burden for her, even bigger than before in her eyes. My father would say before he died, "Eileen all I want to do is look out our front window of our home and watch the people go buy." It never came to be, but something special was uncovered due to my father's death beyond my imagination, I became a licensed social worker specializing in chemical dependency.

While I was working as a RN in the OB?GYN clinic at a city hospital a coincidence occurred. I was the Assistant Director of the clinic, yet I always had a group of people line up to speak to me everyday. Patients young and old with infertility problems, some people diagnosed with cancer and other with high risk pregnancy. I grew close to my patients and they came to me with all kinds of emotional problems. One day a social worker in that area said to me, "You are so talented Eileen why don't you become a social worker. This was when therapy was not so popular and I had no idea what the role of a social worker was. When I questioned her about it she stated I was doing it already doing it without formal education. I worked as an RN full time and attended school at night until I completed my undergraduate and graduate work. While I was attending Adelphi University School of Social Work one of my fellow students, Hal Matthius said, "Do you need a paid field placement? I answered with an excited yes. I was told it was at Freeport Hospital and it specialized in Alcoholism. I responded that I didn't know too much about the subject(major denial). I learned first hand from some of the greatest teachers like Joe Pirro, and Patti Lewis Bobko. Well it was suggested that I attend Al-anon meetings to serve my clients better and that is what began my recovery in the family disease of addiction. Since then I have had the experience in the chemical dependency treatment in hospital based detoxification, halfway houses, outpatient counseling agencies, private practice, and a not for profit agency.

The love for my father, with the help of my higher power, who I call God, has brought me on this path of being the healer of others with God's help. I only wish my father had entered the doors of AA. I remember in the hospital someone in AA came to my father's bed and he wanted to attend AA meetings. I also remember my mother getting a call from someone in Al-anon to attend meetings and she refused, but no one asked me. I wasn't sure what it was all about even though I was an RN in the 1970's. So in his memory I continue to serve the suffering alcoholic/addict and their family members.

Fast forward to 2004 while I was attending an inservice seminar training another student inquired whether I was an author. I responded no, but she was persistent in that she remembered me as a writer. I never had thought about writing and went home to my husband Edward Wolfe and discussed the possibilities of becoming a writer. On month later the wife of an identified patient stated to me that I should write a book about her crazy family. I told her that her family was not crazy and what happened during the intervention I conducted was confidential. She again persisted, but much more forceful than the previous woman and said their were very few books on the internet at that time about interventions and that I should write a book so that more people would understand how vital a technique it is and how I could save more lives. I went home to my husband and said I think God wants me to do something. I was busy with a full-time and part time job and taking care of my children yet I know I had to change something to get this accomplished. Therefore, I stopped my second job and took an online course about nonfiction writing. I started to write my book and wonderful feedback from my fellow students and instructor. I know I had a lot to learn and God would do the rest.

I literately started writing this book on the inside cover of a shoe box since my husband and I were on the road in our RV and I had no paper and ideas were coming to mind. Well God gave me plenty to think about when we went on a business/vacation trip to a four day event in which at least 250,000 people were in the wee hours of the night in close proximity to one another. Many people carried a six pack of beer in a soft cooler. My husband said if you asked any crowd of people anywhere at this event. "Does any one have a can of beer practically anyone would offer you one." Now I had been around heavy drinking most of my childhood and young adult life, but not in such a magnitude or quantity in my life. At first I though nothing of it, "Love and Let Live" and AA, Al-anon slogan. I didn't dare mention what I did for a living. Instead I tried to assist my husband with his business. I met some intelligent, well educated, family minded, patriotic, religious people who were also rowdy, wild and carefree. As the days and nights went on I could count on two hands the amount of sober people that we wanted to befriend for the weekend since we had gone as a couple ourselves.

The vomiting at night occurred close to our motorhome. They boasted about their homes, servants, land and money and their large donations to worthy causes. One was a retired couple that appeared at first, friendly, interesting and very inviting. They sought everyone's friendship and without hesitation offered everyone their hospitality. This hospitality was as much as you wanted to drink in their motorhome while one spouse passed out and the other continue to encourage your companionship.

Some of their food was on the stove cooking endlessly while other food was strewn haphazardly left for those to fend for themselves.

Well we make some causal friends with the sober couples and we make some casual friendships with the heavy drinkers. The one couple I described struck my heart. They were kind, giving, yet so sick. They had asked about my career early on in that evening and I had told them. They described a cousin whose daughter had a drug addiction and was "sent away for six months." She was now in recovery and had a wonderful career. They both were in denial about their past and present drinking episodes with much laughter.

How can one help people who don't see themselves as they really are? There is a way. It is called a Chemical Dependency Family Intervention. You need two family/friends to start an intervention assessment to meet with a professional interventionist. Now in this couple's case their three closes friends died according to them, due to the effects of drinking alcohol. The only chance for this couple would be sober friends/family intervening on them. When I went to sleep that night in our motorhome with the chaos outside I thought about how much work needed to be done in saving lives. I also thought about all the other people that appeared to be drinking heavily four days straight day and night. There were so many in such close quarters that it made such a profound impression on me of the urgency of the matter to start to save as many people as I could. The only way to assist would be dramatically increase the amount of professional interventions we do.

The heavy drinkers there I spoke to told me stories like a matter of fact without even knowing my career. It as if God was speaking through them saying save me. These heavy drinkers during their four days had small children, teenage children and young adults al watching the drunken orgy and was learning quickly to imitate. The adults spoke to perfect strangers about how their children had legal problems due to their drinking and some were being straightened out in the military. While others were just wandering aimlessly in between drinking episodes.

How could I reach the general population of heavy drinkers and ask them to look at themselves and intervene on them? The answer was always interventions. It was staggering to me the amount of work ahead. Besides educating people about their responsibility to catalyze their family members towards taking action towards starting and completing interventions we also need to train more interventionists. There is now a professional association for credentialed interventionists called the Association for Intervention Specialist. This certification is AIS BRI,BRII

My husband and I went to Prescott Arizona and attended two Al-anon meetings while we were there for two weeks. One young couple from AA/Al-anon invited us for dinner in their home to hear about the NY 12 step program. Another older woman asked if we wanted a tour of the town and make us feel welcome. For those of you who don't know that this could be a usual occurrence to have a second meeting at a diner after your local home group has ended that day. We socialize together and learn to live without being addicted to the alcoholic/addict.

Skeptics don't believe in complete abstinence. They don't believe in the 12 step day of life, etc. They ask for statistics from AA/Na, Al-anon, etc. The fact is that the program is anonymous and they don't have statistics. Those skeptics can attend any open AA?na, Al-anon etc meeting or any anniversary of a group or individual. There are also professional 12 step meetings available so the public can witness recovery for themselves.

Just today I was told by an old-timer in AA that he was finally open to the idea of interventions. He stated a good friend told him about it. The caller said he was going to refer a family member in for an intervention assessment. Everyone should have the knowledge about interventions, the man and woman on the street, corporate America, the medical doctor, the clergy, nurses, the guidance counselors, social workers, child protective workers, psychologists, psychiatrists, etc. There should be a pipeline of information and a main list of interventionist. The insurance companies should pay for interventions. It would be a treatment like any other medical treatment known, covered and done. It is a daunting task and I hope I can be the catalyst and provide the continued momentum for that to happen.

Bottom line we are talking about saving lives now and in the future. Are we willing as individuals and as a nation to do what is necessary to make it a reality? Those of you who are please contact me via email. Let's organize. Those of you who want an interventionist call or email me. Hopefully if I get too busy I will give you a list of qualified colleagues so I can refer with the utmost confidence.

Let us all journey together for Recovery in the World. Individual by individual, family by family, community by community, professional by professional. I believe God has a plan for this to happen. Make it happen by asking others to read this book. My next book may be a general overview of what happens after the buzz begins.

Bibliography

Science Practice Perspectives volumes 3 No.1

National Institute on Drug Abuse December 2005 pg 11 and 12

Kolb, Bet 2003. Amphetamine or cocaine limits the ability of later experience to promote structural plasticity in the neocortex and cucleus accumben s. Proceedings of the National academy of Sciences to the United States of America 100(18):10503-10528

Robinson, T.F. and Kolb, 1999 Alterations in the morphology of dentrities and dendtritic spines in the nucleus accumbens and prefrontal cortex following repeated treatment with amphetamine aor cocaine. Eurpoean Jouornal of Neuro Science 11:1598-1604

Al-anon Alateen Service manual 1998-2000 pg 24 Al-anon Family Group Headquarters Inc. 1992 pg 16

Al-anon slogans Courage to Change pg 16, pg 23, pg 30

Roots and Wings Parenting Program Hazelden Publishing Company pg 11

Resources

AIS Association of Intervention Specialist
Execusuites
15200 Shady Grove Road MD 20850
www.intervention.com/AISMembers/

AA World Service
Grand Central Station
PO Box 459 NY NY 10163
212 8703400

Narcotics Anonymous World Service
PO Box 9999
Van Nuys, CA 91409
818 7739999

Al-Anon/Al-Ateen World Service
1600 Corporate Landing Parkway
Virginia Beach, VA 23454-5617
757 5631600
1888 4252666
www.al-anon.alateen.org

The Substance Abuse and Mental Health Services Administration
Office of Communication
301 4438956
1800 662 help
www.samhsa.gov

National Institute of Alcohol Abuse and Alcoholism
NIAAA Department of Health and Human Services
310 4433885
www.niaaa.n.h.gov

Employee Assistance Professional Association (EAP)
703 387 1000
www.eap-assocciation.com

Hazelden Publishing Company

Hazelden
15245 Pleasant Valley Road
Center City, MN 55012
www.hazelden.org

Dr. Ohlm
PO BOX 410363
St. Louis, Missouri 63141

National Council on Alcoholism and Drug Dependence
244 East 58th Street
4th Floor
NY, NY 10022
212 269 7797

The author shall have neither liability nor responsibility to any person or entity with respect to any loss or damage caused or alleged to have been directly, indirectly by the information in this book (This message was taken as a protection and found in another book in print to protect the author) I in no way want to plagiarize I just want to protect myself. This specific paragraph is not of my own wording it is just used as protection and I mean no harm to the other author that has used this wording.

516 4586962
Author contact
Eileen Wolfe
Email edsoil34 @aol.com
Books and libraries